For Lydia, Abigail, and Margaret Huck
F. P. H.

For Emma Horne
J. F.

Text copyright © 1969, 2000 by Florence Parry Heide
Illustrations copyright © 2000 by Jules Feiffer

First edition 2000

Library of Congress Cataloging-in-Publication Data

Heide, Florence Parry.
Some things are scary / Florence Parry Heide ; illustrated by Jules Feiffer. — 1st ed.
p. cm.
Summary: A list of scary things includes "skating downhill when you haven't learned
how to stop, getting hugged by someone you don't like," and "finding out your
best friend has a best friend who isn't you."
ISBN 0-7636-1222-7 (hardcover)
[1. Fear — Fiction.] I. Feiffer, Jules, ill. II. Title.
PZ7.H36 SI 2000
[E] — dc21
00-025921

2 4 6 8 10 9 7 5 3 1

Printed in the United States of America

This book was typeset in Soupbone.
The illustrations were done in watercolor with felt-tip marker.

Candlewick Press
2067 Massachusetts Avenue
Cambridge, Massachusetts 02140

Some Things Are

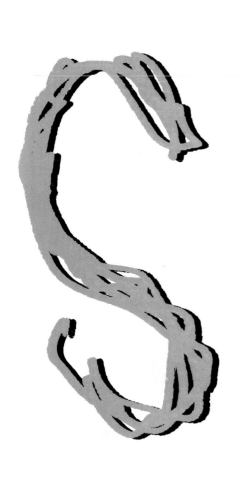 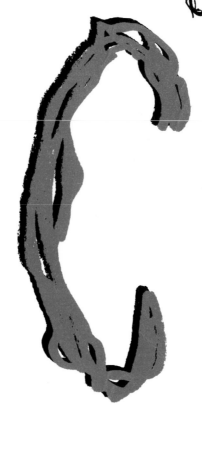 

S C A

CANDLEWICK PRESS
CAMBRIDGE, MASSACHUSETTS

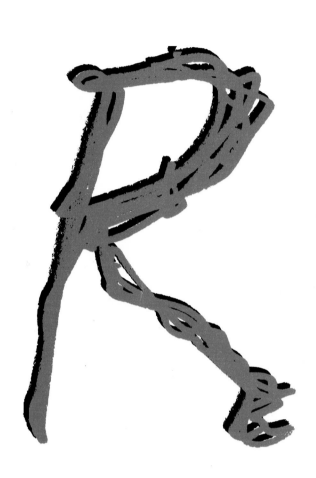
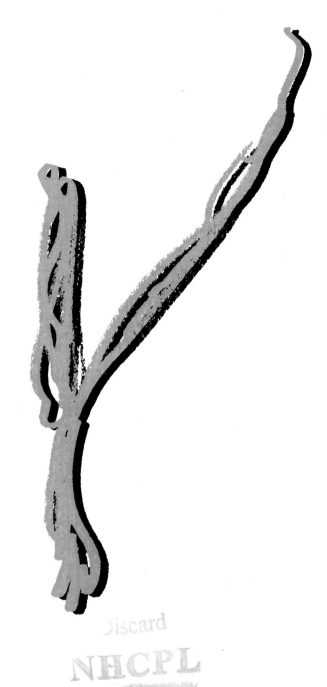

Florence Parry Heide

illustrated by Jules Feiffer

Getting hugged by someone you don't like

is scary.

Seeing something on your plate
you know you're not going to like

is scary.

Stepping on something
squishy when you're in
your bare feet

is scary.

Holding on to someone's hand
that isn't your mother's when
you thought it was

is scary.

Seeing a big warning sign
and you can't understand
what it's saying

is scary.

Skating downhill when you haven't learned how to stop

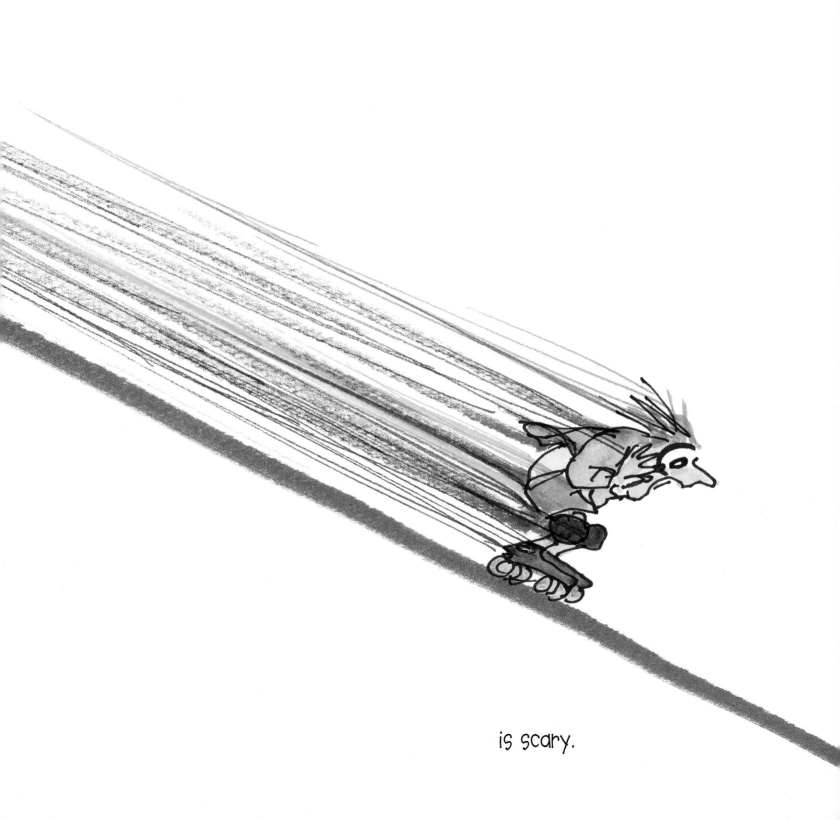

is scary.

Waiting to jump out
and say BOO!
at someone

Knowing that someone
is waiting to jump out and
say BOO! at you

is scary.

is scary.

Being on a swing when someone is pushing you too high

is scary.

Getting a shot

is scary.

Telling a lie

is scary.

Stepping down from something that is higher than you thought it was

Smelling a flower and finding a bee was smelling it first

is scary.

is scary.

Being with your mother when she can't remember where she parked the car

is scary.

Discovering that your hamster cage is empty

is scary.

Getting scolded

is scary.

Finding out your best friend has a best friend who isn't you

Playing hide-and-seek when you're it and you can't find anyone

Having your best friend move away

is scary.

Thinking about a big bird with big teeth
who might swoop down and carry you away

is scary.

Brushing your teeth with something you thought was toothpaste but it isn't

is scary.

Reaching under your bed for your shoes and grabbing something — you don't know what —

is scary.

Thinking you're never going to get any taller than you are right now

is scary.

Having to tell someone your name and they can't understand you and you have to spell it

is scary.

Knowing your parents are talking about you and you can't hear what they're saying

is scary.

Having people looking at you and
laughing and you don't know why

is scary.

Climbing a tree
when you don't
remember how
to get down

is scary.

Being with your parents in an art museum and thinking you're never going to see the exit sign

is scary.

Knowing
you're going
to grow up
to be a
grownup

is
scary.